GUIDE TO GOOD HAIRDRESSING

GUIDE TO GOOD HAIRDRESSING

A fun, quick, informative guide to choosing
and exploring your career potential in the
hairdressing industry.

JULIE HANDLEY

JANUS PUBLISHING COMPANY
London, England

Janus Publishing Company Ltd,
105-107 Gloucester Place
London W1U 6BU

www.januspublishing.co.uk

British Library Cataloguing-in-publication Data
A catalogue record for this book is
available from the British Library

ISBN 1 85756 544 4

Cover Design: Simon Hughes

Printed and bound in Great Britain

About the Author

Where I started

I left school at sixteen to pursue my chosen career as a hair-dresser. The school careers adviser had suggested I join a YTS (Youth Training Scheme), where I would be given an apprenticeship for two years. I was then given a list of hair salons to contact in order to find a sponsor.

I contacted five salon chains in Leeds, my home town, and two replied! One of these was a well-known and respected international salon chain. They sent me an application form, wanting to know what my career aspirations were, why I'd an interest in them and what I knew about the company.

I returned the form and shortly afterwards I received a letter asking me to attend an interview. The first stage was as a group, telling us about the company, asking us questions to see how assertive we were, etc. The second stage was a short one-to-one, where they wanted to know why I wanted the job and how committed I was prepared to be. I finally got the job!

I worked as a junior during the day and trained three evenings a week. I earned £29 a week the first year and £32 the second! Although I was trained in all areas, I specialised in colour and perm and after two years I qualified as a colour and perm specialist.

Once qualified, I had the opportunity to work in their salons all over the UK. I earned between £500 and £800 a month, depending on how busy I was (that wasn't too bad for a late 80s salary!), and at the very least £10 a day in tips.

Other roles I experienced

Freelance

I left the above organisation to work for some friends who had opened their own salon in London. I worked for them on a freelance basis, enjoying flexible hours. This allowed me to return to college – whilst still earning my living in the salon. I did this for three years and was able to study art, art history and practical computing skills.

Manufacturer

After I had completed my courses, I decided to throw myself back into a full-time progressive hairdressing career. I contacted one of the haircare giants and after two interviews was fortunate to be employed as a trainer. After six weeks of intense training myself, I then taught young and inexperienced hairdressers in product knowledge and usage. I visited salons where colours had gone wrong (blonde hair had turned green!) and supported the hairdresser by offering guidance in how to rectify it. My salary and benefits package improved greatly.

Working for a manufacturer gave me the opportunity to achieve my NVQ (National Vocational Qualification) Level 3, which is the equivalent of an A-level and is well recognised in the industry. I also became an assessor of candidates and their trainers. I was there for six years, until I finally left London and moved to Cambridgeshire.

College lecturer

I decided to formalise my training experience by enrolling for my teacher training qualification. As I trained for this in the evenings, I also taught and demonstrated hairdressing theory and skills to school-leavers and returners at the city college. I achieved my qualification certificate and had the pleasure of teaching a wonderful, talented group of aspiring hairdressers! Being a lecturer was well paid on an hourly basis and the hours were more flexible.

Today

I freelance, doing my regular customers - and of course family and friends! This has been a very rewarding career that has allowed me to explore different avenues and taught me new things in the process. I have had some very hard and some very good times, and met some fun and interesting customers and friends.

What have I gained from the haircare industry?

Hairdressing skills that I will have for life:

* A hairdresser will never be out of work for long!
* Have met and done celebrities' hair.
* Hair colour for weekly magazines and a hair colour book.
* Won runner-up junior colourist award with well-known organisation.
* Won trainer of the year with haircare manufacturer.
* An NVQ Level 3 formal qualification.
* D32 and D33 formal assessing qualifications.
* A formal teaching qualification.
* Experience in salons, training and freelance work.
* Knowledge and experience to write this book and hopefully encourage and help aspiring hairdressers.

With the fifteen years' experience I have gained, I am currently looking to open my own hairdressing businesses. I would recommend this rewarding and exciting industry to anyone with a passion for hairdressing!

Contents

Introduction

What does a career in hairdressing mean to you? Is it working in a salon (on the shop floor), is it specialising in areas such as Afro-Caribbean hair, colouring, cutting? Maybe you want to aspire to be famous, like Nicky Clarke, Beverly Cobella and John Frieda. Or perhaps you're a born teacher and you want to impart your knowledge and experience to develop new aspiring hairdressers as a college lecturer/salon trainer?

Whatever this career means to you, a few things are for sure - it's a diverse, energetic industry and you will need to be prepared to work hard. There will be people who will teach and inspire you and those who try your patience and test your people and communication skills!

It's also a lot of fun; you'll make some great friends on the way and you'll be working within the fashion industry. Once you have worked hard to qualify as a fully trained hairdresser you have many avenues to explore and develop if you want to:

Hairdresser – has all-round skills.

Hair stylist – specialises in ladies' haircutting.

Barber – specialises in men's haircutting.

Technician – colour and perm specialist.

Afro-Caribbean specialist – specialises in Afro-Caribbean/black hair types.

Long hair specialist – hairdressing hair for weddings/hair extensions.

College lecturer.

Mobile hairdresser – visiting clients at home.

Trainer/salesperson – for a haircare manufacturer.
Session work – for TV, magazines, catalogues, fashion shows, etc.

When you have completed your training and you are fully qualified, the skills you have spent years learning and developing will stay with you for life. A hairdresser will always be in demand. A hairdresser will never be out of work.

So why are you looking to choose a career in hairdressing?

Chapter One

Why choose a career in hairdressing?

I put emphasis on the word "choose" as I once heard that hairdressing was for school-leavers with no qualifications! This, apparently, was an easy option in order to push an uncertain candidate into a job when he or she left school.

Anyone who thinks this is an easy industry is very misguided! A lot of hard work and diplomacy skills are required, as you are constantly dealing with people - from colleagues to the salon clientele. You will need to have a lot of energy, smile and be polite, and you cannot afford to have a bad day in front of the customer - therefore, to choose this career you have to have the right mindset and not take the job because you think of it as an easy option: it isn't.

There are a lot of salons that will be prepared to employ, train and develop you. In return you may be working as a trainee, where you will look after clients, help the stylists by shampooing and preparing the customers' hair, make the tea/coffee and be instrumental in maintaining salon cleanliness. Yes, it's just a starting point, but it's an important one in order to build confidence in handling customers and different hair types. You will need this experience and knowledge to further your own career in the longer term.

This is a realistic, people-oriented industry and the reasons you should be choosing this career are:

- You like people!
- You are friendly and polite.
- You want to do well and work hard.
- You want to learn new skills - not just hair-related, but communication skills too.
- You believe in good customer care and customer satisfaction.
- You have a thirst for knowledge.
- You are interested in what you are doing.*

Where do I start?

To help you make your very important decision in joining the hairdressing industry, you could contact salons near to where you live and ask for work experience placements.

Work experience

This means asking if you could help out after school hours, on Saturdays or during school holidays. If you have left school, then it may be worth asking for two weeks' work experience.

This experience will be a taste of what will be expected when you first start work in a hair salon (see Chapter Two). You will be expected to do the following.

- Greet clients, take their coats and offer them a salon gown.
- Show them to their seat/offer refreshments.
- Shampoo (if you've been taught this - however, this will not always be the case initially).
- Sweep the floor, tidy the work positions, refill shampoo bottles, etc.
- Assist the stylists/colourists when requested.

- Work experience is usually unpaid - however, you may earn tips from clients you've shampooed, brought tea/coffee to, etc.

Once you have completed your work experience, your careers adviser can give advice and details of school-leavers' schemes and hairdressing colleges you can apply to. If you have left school or are in employment but looking for a career change, you can proactively contact salons in your area and ask if they will give you an apprenticeship.

Salons will always require juniors/assistants in order to train and develop the next level of up-and-coming hairdressers. Salon owners and managers know that it is those hairdressers with the right attitude and skills who will encourage new and loyal customers to their business. The best advertising is word of mouth and it is well known that a bad word will often get around quicker than a good one.

What will salon owners look for?

Personal qualities
- Good positive attitude.
- Commitment - working in a salon requires some evenings and Saturdays.
- Friendliness and politeness - as you will be dealing with the salon's customers.
- Willingness to learn and progress - they will want to train you to be the next level of hairdresser in the event that a stylist leaves or there are more clients and not enough staff.
- A hardworking attitude and assertiveness.

How you present yourself

You may be required to wear a uniform to project the salon image

* If not, you will still need to look smart and professional, with spotlessly clean clothes and good personal hygiene.
* Your hair will need to be shampooed daily, again to project a good salon image - after all, you will be a walking advert for them!
* You will need to wear comfortable shoes, as being on your feet is all part of the job.
* Hands should be clean and nails well trimmed.

A bit about you

They will want to understand your personality and assess whether you are the right person to fit into their salon ethics and existing team. To help them understand you and what you can do, it is a good idea to put together a CV (curriculum vitae). The CV is for you to record information that will be of interest to a new employer. It is a summary of achievement and will help them build up a picture of your attitude, skills and experience. Normally a CV will provide the following information.

* Name, address, contact numbers.
* Short profile on yourself, e.g. your experience to date in a nutshell.
* Career history, starting from the most recent date.
* Achievements to date, e.g. promotions/winning awards.
* Training/qualifications you have.
* Personal interests.

If you have recently left school then you can't possibly have done a lot of the above yet, so as a guide you may want to include the following.

- Name, address, contact numbers.
- Short profile on yourself.
- Work experience, if any.
- School qualifications.
- Personal interests.

An example CV is set out to your right.

Your Name
Your Address
Your phone number(s) and e-mail address

Profile

I am a 16-year old school-leaver looking to fulfil my ambition as a hair-dresser. While at school, I worked as a Saturday girl at my local salon for three months. Prior to that, I had three weeks' work experience at a well-known hairdressing chain in the centre of town. I am prepared to work hard and I enjoy learning.

Work Experience

Super Cuts   Jan '03 to Mar '03
Worked on Saturdays, the busiest day of the week. This involved seating clients ready for the stylist, shampooing, organising the stock and generally maintaining the high level of cleanliness of the salon.

Toni & Guy   July '02 to Aug '02
I had three full weeks learning the skills needed to offer good customer care. I learnt how to shampoo properly and watched many demonstrations in blow-drying and cutting.

Qualifications

Art & Design   -   Grade
English   -   Grade
Maths   -   Grade
Etc.

Personal Interests

I am currently learning to drive
Enjoy sports and the gym
Like socialising and meeting new people
Painting and sketching*
Etc.

Some salons you might write to or phone will send you their own application form, on which you can record any experience, however little, that you have had. If you are changing your career to join the hairdressing industry, then previous employment, skills and training are still very relevant.

Interview

Once you have made contact with the salon, you will hopefully be invited to an interview. If not, there are plenty more salons - keep trying!

The interview could be a one-to-one with the salon owner/manager or it could be a group interview (where the salon is looking to employ a certain number of new aspiring hairdressers in one go).

One-to-one

If you are offered an interview in writing, the letter will tell you the date, time and place to attend. If it is by phone then they will tell you the best time to meet with them, or you will need to ask. Whichever, you will need to ensure the following.

- If you are unsure where the venue is, try and find it a few days earlier so you know where you are going on the day and how long it will take you.
- Make sure you are on time!
- Make sure you are smart and professional-looking, i.e. don't go dressed as if you are going clubbing!
- Take your CV, however short, as this will show assertiveness. If they have sent you an application form for you to complete then take that to show that you have prepared.
- Pre-prepare some questions for them, e.g. how many staff work there (this will show the size of the organisation), what their training structure is (this will show you the salon's com-

mitment in staff investment), how many hours they want you to work, and what is the pay, holiday entitlement, etc.

* Don't be afraid to ask questions, as this will show that you are interested and will make sure you are prepared to meet the salon requirements.

Group interview

If the salon (usually larger organisations) is looking for a new junior/assistant intake, you will probably be sent an application form first and then notified as to whether you have an interview. The group interview may be where they inform you about their organisation, the job role and the training and development they will give you.

The group may be asked questions afterwards, which will tell the prospective employers who is showing interest. Even if you are a shy person, the fact that you at least try to answer questions will be demonstrated to the employer.

After the group interview, there will possibly be a one-to-one, where they will want to know more about you as an individual. Other questions you may be asked in an interview situation are:

* Why do you want to be a hairdresser?
* What do you know about our organisation?
* Where do you see yourself in three years?
* What qualities/experience do you have to bring to this role?
* What are your strengths and weaknesses?

Employers will want to see how committed you are likely to be and what your expectations are. The fact that you know something about their organisation shows that you are keen enough to have done your homework. For example, you may have visited their website to see if the salon has done any glossy magazine work or taken part in any of the big industry awards. It may be that they are a very well-known chain that has a reputation for excellent cutting work and training structure. It could be a smaller salon that is always busy and you would like to be part of a close-knit team.

With questions about your strengths and weaknesses, you may want to ask your family and friends what they think before going to the interview. Strengths could be that you get on well with people, you're organised, eager and quick to learn. Weaknesses could be that you need to watch your time-keeping, but that you are aware that this needs to become a strength!

When choosing weaknesses, make sure you back them up with how you are going to correct them and turn them into strengths. Don't be afraid to be honest - employers like honesty and realise that everybody has weaknesses, however experienced they may be.

Conclusion

This career will be hard work and you will need to want to learn and do well. In return it will be fun, you will meet some creative, interesting and lively people on the way, and above all else it will be rewarding by giving you lifelong skills and the opportunity to explore different avenues during your chosen career.

Chapter Two

What should I expect when I get there?

OK, so you've completed your work experience, contacted the salon you would like to work in, had an interview, and demonstrated your assertiveness and preparation skills. You've filled in the application form/CV and pre-prepared questions to ask.

Maybe it's your first attempt at gaining employment, maybe you've already had a few interviews previously - whichever, you've got the job and now you need an idea of what to expect when you get there.

All salons will vary, from being a small, busy salon with one or two stylists to medium-sized established salons with five or more staff, to the larger chains, which may have twenty to thirty staff in hair salons in major cities. Whichever you work in, your role to begin with will be similar in each. The structure I refer to below will also differ, but will give you an idea as to what you can aspire to.

Your role

- You will be there to assist the stylists in client care, such as greeting at reception, gowning, seating and offering refreshments. Many customers visit the salon to be pampered and for a treat - therefore it is important that their treatment is as pleasurable as possible (imagine the kind of service you expect and would like improved when you visit a restaurant, clothes shop, or wherever).

- You will be expected to smile and be friendly, even if you don't feel like it! Clients also come to the salon to remove themselves from their everyday life, especially if there are problems. Many hairdressers say that their clients talk to them on a personal basis, on which they build a good relationship that can last years.*
- Customers visit a salon that has a clean, hygienic and comfortable environment. Part of your role is to ensure the floor is free from hair, that workstations are polished and hair products are neatly placed. Towels, gowns, combs and brushes need to be clean and dry and ready for the stylist to use. It's a bit like when you or I go to a sandwich bar or restaurant - we don't want to see dirty plates left around, stained table cloths or food particles on the floor!
- In some cases, you may be required to answer the phone and book appointments. The salon will train you in how they want the phone answered and how the appointments are to be spaced throughout the day.
- Making tea and coffee.
- Shampooing. You will need to assess the customer's hair type and select the appropriate shampoo and conditioner to make their hair feel clean, healthy and well prepared for the stylist. You may need to know how to do head massages as an additional luxury for the customer. The towel may have to be wrapped in a certain way to stop the customer's hair from dripping.

Structure
Salon owner
Salon manager/assistant manager
Art director/in-salon trainers
Senior stylists/colourists and permers
Top stylists/colourists and permers

Junior stylists/colourists and returners
Senior juniors/assistants
Juniors/assistants
Work experience/Saturday helpers

Salon owner

They may also work in the salon and have their own clientele as well as managing the staff, costs, dealing with any complaints, etc.

Salon manager/assistant manager

They work for the owner and are responsible for the smooth running of the salon, staff welfare, analysing daily, weekly and monthly takings, buying haircare products, and dealing with complaints.

Art director

In larger organisations the art director may be involved in magazine or show work and will lead the salon in creating new looks, e.g. new haircuts, colours or perm techniques. Examples of hair fashion leaders are Vidal Sassoon, Toni & Guy, Beverly Cobbella and Nicky Clarke.

In-salon trainers

They may again have their own clientele, but they spend a certain amount of time with new members of staff, demonstrating haircutting, colouring, perming, long-hair techniques, and so on. They may offer coaching to more experienced staff who need to develop a certain area or who are close to qualifying.

Senior stylists/colourists

Usually staff who have established clients of their own. It is a promotion to reward them for their hard work and level of experience. There is also a pricing structure within the average salon tariff and the senior stylist/colourist will charge more than the junior member of staff.

Junior stylists/colourists and returners
Newly qualified staff or returners (those who've had a break from hairdressing) who are starting to build their own clientele from scratch. I make reference to "building" a clientele as no one can assume they will automatically inherit customers. There are many salons a customer can go to; they do not have to come to you - they choose to.

Senior juniors/assistants
Juniors who are established in their role and are being developed in new areas, e.g. from shampooing and blow-drying to basic cutting and colouring. These are the juniors who will soon progress to the junior stylist.

Juniors/assistants
Newer members who will be instrumental in ensuring that the salon is clean and tidy and that customers are well looked after. They will also shampoo and do preparation work, as they progress towards becoming senior juniors/assistants.

Work experience/Saturday helpers
This will give you the opportunity to gain some experience of what to expect in the early stages of your career. It will also show your eventual permanent employer that you are serious about your role.

Chapter Three

Roles outside the salon

Mobile hairdresser

Once you have qualified from your salon training or college, you may want to be the mobile hairdresser that visits people's homes. You will need a car or access to good public transport. You will need your working tools such as scissors, combs, brushes and hairdryer. You will also need to buy styling products and colour and permanent wave solutions, as you won't have access to the products routinely stocked by a salon.

The mobile hairdresser may still work (or have previously worked) in a salon and have had requests from customers who are no longer able to visit the salon. These could be elderly and infirm customers or new mums, for example, as well as your friends and family.

College lecturer

To be a lecturer, you must be fully qualified and ideally have a good level of experience, as you will be influencing younger, aspiring hairdressers. You may be required to have a formal teaching qualification prior to becoming a lecturer, although some colleges will allow you to achieve this qualification as you fulfil the teaching role.

You will also need to have your NVQ (National Vocational Qualification) Level 3 in hairdressing skills and service. Part of your role as a lecturer will be to teach the theory of hair science, products and skills as well as demonstrate them. You will also need to use coaching skills when your students have their own models to work on.

When your students have a good understanding of a subject such as full head colouring, then they can start applying and choosing colours on live models (usually family and friends at first!). They will be required to do a series of assessments which count towards the NVQ qualification. These are a set of standards the student has to achieve and which count towards their competence as a fully fledged hairdresser.

Working for a haircare manufacturer

Should you wish to develop your training and selling skills, you will need to be fully qualified and with good experience in salon work and client care. Haircare manufacturers have trainers to support their customers in product knowledge and usage - after all, a product is only as good as its user. The more hairdressers know and understand about a product, the more confident they will be in using it. If they have had, or seen, a bad experience and lost confidence in a product, it will no doubt gather dust in a cupboard!

Manufacturers also need salespeople to visit salons and introduce them to new products and encourage the sales of existing ones. Usually previous sales experience is required and a hairdressing background is not always necessary.

Examples of hair care manufactures are *Wella*, *L'oreal*, *Schwartcof* and *Goldwell*.

Session stylist

This could be a hairdresser who is working freelance (not employed by a salon but working for themselves), relying on industry contacts for work such as hair for magazine shoots, TV and fashion events.

To be a session stylist, you will usually need to have a good portfolio of work (good quality photographs projecting a total image from hair to clothes, make-up and background). Have a look in some of the glossy magazines for examples. The photographs you see do not show just hair or just clothes, they show a total image. A session stylist will also usually have built up a good supply of contacts so they will be in demand.

Conclusion

Once you are qualified, you have many choices as to which area of your career you would like to develop. Keep learning, keep your skills and ideas fresh. Well-known stylists who have gone on to open their own salon chains or work on TV all had to start somewhere.

Chapter Four

What will I be paid?

Junior/assistant

As a junior/assistant, you will receive a set wage, usually paid weekly. Although this is sometimes not very well paid, you will have the opportunity to earn tips from your shampooing/client care. Some salons allow all members of staff to keep their own tips; some encourage a tip box so they can be shared between all staff at the end of the day.

Stylist/colourist

Once you qualify and start to build your clientele, you will be paid a salary monthly, which will probably be a set basic with the opportunity to earn commission. This means you are given a fixed amount, with commission on top, e.g. if you achieve a certain number of haircuts you get an extra amount in your pay packet. You may also earn money on top of your basic monthly salary if you recommend more customers for having colour.

Self-employed

If you are self employed, which is more commonly known in the salon as "rent-a-chair", you will give the salon owner an agreed percentage of your takings. This covers the overheads, such as lighting, equipment, water and products. It may also cover your insurance.

It is recommended that you see an accountant or new business adviser at your chosen bank. They will guide you on the following.

- Opening a business account into which you pay your earnings and from which you pay your work-related costs.
- Buy an account book and keep a record of all income and outgoings in separate columns. Keep the receipts for all your work-related outgoings.
- Record your daily, weekly and monthly takings.
- Record how much you then pay back to the salon owner.
- Record any expenses you have incurred, e.g. if you have had to buy certain products that the salon doesn't stock or hair decoration for a special occasion.
- Keep this record for tax purposes.
- If you are a mobile hairdresser, you should also keep statements and any information regarding your earnings and outgoings.
- Use this information when you are completing your tax returns.
- Don't forget to still pay your National Insurance! Otherwise you could end up with a large backdated bill!

Remember, when you are self-employed, you do not get paid for sickness, maternity or holidays; therefore managing your money is essential.

Conclusion
Once you have gained your experience, you have the opportunity to progress further and earn a decent living. You will have the skills to build and maintain a good clientele - more clients means more money. These skills are your living and will be with you for life.

Chapter Five

Communication skills

What is communication?
Communicating allows us to give and receive information via different methods, e.g. verbally, written and visually.

Before we go into the key communication areas for hairdressers, which are usually verbal and visual, there is another essential skill we must learn to do well - listen. Listening to what the customer actually wants rather than what we think they want is essential if you are to build a successful clientele.

Verbal communication – how we speak, what we say

Voice tone
How we say things is important. We can say the same word with different tones of voice and the listener can interpret these differently, e.g. try saying the word "yes" in the following ways.

- Enthusiastically.
- With reluctance.
- Positively/in agreement.
- Impatiently.

It's the same word, but because it's said with a different tone of voice, it can actually mean "no" or "yes, but I don't want to!"

Voice strength

How loud or softly we speak. We need to pitch our voice strength to our listener, e.g. if you speak too softly and the listener has to keep asking you to repeat what you are saying, they are eventually going to switch off - therefore what you are trying to say won't be heard.

If you are too loud, this could be perceived as too impersonal to the listener, e.g. talking loudly in a quieter salon where everyone can overhear may mean the listener won't respond well through feeling exposed.

Terminology

The words we use enable the listener to understand - or not understand in some cases. Terminology or jargon are words specific to an area or industry, and therefore are not always common words and phrases that everyone would know, e.g.:

Soft perm - the customer may describe the perm they want as being "soft". To the hairdresser, this could mean a wavy perm that will last a few weeks. To the customer this could mean a perm that has firm curls - but it will feel soft in condition.

The colour red - the customer could see this as pillar-box red. To the hairdresser, there are many shades of red, from dark, rich mahogany red, chestnut red, rich copper, etc.

Blonde - the customer could imagine bleached, white highlights. The hairdresser could be meaning a pale golden blonde.

Questioning techniques

Questioning techniques are a verbal method of extracting information and encouraging people to talk. There are quite a few questioning techniques, such as open, closed, ambiguous, probing, multiple. The two you are most likely to use with your customers are "open" and "closed" questions, which we look at below.

Open questions

This is asking a question in a way that cannot be answered with "yes" or "no". Open questions can be asked in the following way:

* How are you feeling today? (Cannot be answered with "yes" or "no" so the person has to give you some indication as to how they are feeling.)
* When did you last have your hair cut?
* Where are you going on holiday?
* What are you planning for the weekend?
* Why are you unsure about having a perm?

Closed questions

These can be seen as negative as they can give us limited information or close down conversation, as they can only be answered with "yes" or "no", and you then have to work harder to find another question to keep the conversation moving. E.g.:

* Do you feel OK today?
* Did you have your hair cut here the last time?
* Have you been on holiday?
* Are you planning anything for the weekend?
* Would you have a perm again?

Practise these two questioning techniques on your family and friends and see how you can open up conversation or close it down!

Although closed questions can sometimes be seen as negative, they can also have a positive side, e.g. if you have informed your customer of the correct after-care products he or she needs to purchase for their hair, and the customer is showing "buying signals" (showing interest by asking questions/reading the back of bottles) you can close the sale by asking a closed question:

+ Would you like me to organise these products at reception for you?
+ Would you like to buy these today? I can show you how to use them now.

Non-verbal communication

Body language
This is something we all use, whoever we are communicating with. Certain things we do can give the person we're communicating with an idea of how receptive/hostile we are being, e.g.:

+ The listener looking at everything but the person talking can indicate they are uninterested in what is being said.
+ The listener who gives good eye contact and nods occasionally is attentive and showing interest/agreement.
+ The person who has their arms tightly folded and chin tucked low can show resistance, hostility and disagreement.
+ Someone who is sitting at ease can be more receptive.

There are books that explain how to analyse body language, which proves what a vast subject it is. Try having a conversation with a friend without moving your head, arms, eyes, body

- it's virtually impossible! Observe each other's body language and start to build up a picture of behaviours.

Eye contact

When communicating with customers, it's important to try to have an even level of eye contact. Have you ever been in a salon where you sat facing the mirror and the stylist was talking to you through the mirror? Did it make you want to try to turn round to face the stylist? Did it feel comfortable and personal? When you are a stylist, the best thing to do is bring a cutting stool over and sit beside the customer so you are face to face, with level eye contact.

Eye contact should be relaxed and not too intense (they don't want to feel interrogated!). Having too little eye contact (you are glancing around the salon all the time to see what else is going on) can show a lack of interest and concentration on your part.

Demonstration

There is only so much that we can understand verbally. This is why actually watching someone cut hair, apply a colour or massage the head in a certain way can be an effective way to learn. When in the salon, if it is a quiet period, it is not unusual for junior members of staff to stand at a comfortable distance, while watching the stylist cut, blow-dry and generally handle the customer's hair. This unstaged demonstration can pass on valuable tips to the learner. For a trainer to demonstrate a haircut and verbally explain it is even better.

Visual aids

Visual aids as a means to communicating with customers are a key method, especially if they are going for a dramatic change, e.g. long hair cut short or going to blonde from naturally dark hair. The customer will sometimes bring in a photograph or magazine cutting of the style or colour she wants you to achieve. This gives you an idea of what her interpretations are and you can manage her expectations as to whether the look is achievable on her hair type.

Conclusion

We need to be skilled in many ways as a hairdresser. We need to learn hair-related skills and how to give a good service, yes, but we also need to be excellent communicators in the process. Look how many salons are on the local high street and in the town centre or city - usually quite a few. Customers are spoilt for choice and do not have to come to your salon - they choose to depending on the service they receive, the atmosphere they can relax in and the way they are treated by the staff.

Chapter Six

Consultation (using your communication skills)

What is a consultation?

This is where we establish what the customer's expectations are and where we impart our professional knowledge and experience in order to meet those expectations.

When does this take place?

This can be with a new customer who has just walked in wanting some ideas for a new look with a view to booking an appointment. It is also one of the very first conversations before any hair services have been performed and at the very end when the service is complete and you are advising on after-care.

What do I do? What do I ask?

- When you have greeted your customer and introduced yourself (if he or she is new to you), pull up a stool and sit, as suggested previously, beside the customer, face to face with level eye contact.
- Use your open questioning techniques to establish what he or she is expecting today, e.g.:* trim, restyle, blow-dry, full head colour, highlights, perm, etc.
- If the customer is looking for a change, suggest styles that would suit her. If she is unsure, use visual aids such as other people in the salon, magazines or hair-styling guides.

- If she is looking to have a colour or a perm, use the shade guide and style guides.
- If she has ideas of her own and wants blonde highlights, for example, find out what her interpretation of blonde is. Ask her if she imagines golden blonde, pale blonde or strawberry blonde. Show her how these look in the shade guide, maybe suggest two different complementary blondes - this is personalising her look and offering her something unique.
- After you have completed the service, suggest haircare products that will maintain colour and condition.

What else do I need to consider?

As a hairdresser, you will also need to look at your customer's hair from a technical viewpoint, taking into consideration the following.

- Condition, texture and porosity (don't worry if you are not familiar with these terms, they will be explained in Chapter Nine).
- Scalp condition.
- Outgrown colour or perm.
- Existing hairstyle and length.
- Face shape and skin tone.
- Are colour, perm and hairstyle achievable on the hair type?

Customers come to us for professional advice on what will make them look their very best. Have you ever seen someone with a haircut that doesn't suit their face shape or a colour that is unsuitable for the skin tone? For example:

Wrong haircut - can exaggerate a strong jaw line, make a round face rounder, a long face longer.

Right haircut - it won't stop a round face being round, but it will complement it so it doesn't exaggerate it any further!

Wrong colour - can make the face look deathly pale, eyes can look shadowy, it can look like unnatural hair*.

Right colour - it looks like real hair, brings out the warm skin tones, making the customer look healthy. If the skin tone is cooler, then it works with this and doesn't make it too pale-looking. The right colour will not exaggerate any dark shadows around the eyes/cheekbones and it will complement the eyebrow colour and any freckles.

Conclusion
The consultation is for the customer and hairdresser to agree the services and results to be achieved. It is also for the hairdresser to assess the hair, skin and image of the customer and advise on the right style and/or colour to complement them. Anyone can purchase hair colourants from shops, which means customers do not have to come to you any more to have their grey hair covered or highlights in their hair. In a lot of cases home colourants are successful, but when they're not, it's you who will need to correct it, which is why you have to establish:

+ What the customer is looking for.
+ What they currently have on their hair.
+ What can realistically be achieved.

Chapter Seven

Relationships

Customers

These relationships earn you your living.

When you are a junior/assistant, customers will get to know you on a regular basis; they'll remember how courteous you are, the good shampoo you give, the fact you care about what you are doing. Once you are qualified, they will possibly stick with you as one of your own clients for cutting, colouring, perming, etc.

A client isn't loyal to a salon just because of the stylist/colourist: it is also down to how they are handled on the phone and by you. You make a difference to the quality of their experience.

When you are qualified and building your own clientele, you will need to ensure you are offering an excellent service - you cannot rely on the fact that customers will come to you regardless.

Building a clientele for the first time

- Have a list of customers booked in with you that day. Be aware of their names and the service they have booked in for.
- When the customer arrives, greet them by their name. This is more personal.
- If you are running late, acknowledge that they have arrived, offer them refreshments and let them know you

are going to be ten or fifteen minutes. This way they are not feeling anxious that they've been forgotten and also they are aware of how long they are going to be in the salon. Some customers could have their car on a meter or need to get back to work.

- When you are ready, make sure your workstation is free from hair, tissues, hair colourant and used coffee cups*.

- Greet the customer by their name, hang up their coat, help them on with their gown and offer them a seat.

- Once they are seated, remember your communication skills. Don't talk to them through the mirror! Pull up a seat or cutting stool next to the customer, face to face, with eye contact comfortable and level.

- Ask them what they are looking for today - establish whether it is a cut, colour, perm, blow-dry or whatever. If you need to, use visuals such as the colour shade guide, magazines or other styles on staff within the salon to help you communicate with your customer.

- Once the customer has been shampooed and you are cutting, be aware of whether your customer wants to talk, read a magazine or sit with their own thoughts.

- Once completed, ask your customer how it feels. Let them hold the hand mirror while you turn the chair to the front so they have a good view of the back.

- Remove the gown so they can see their newly vamped look with their own image.

- Take the trouble to show your customer to reception, ask her if she needs any of the haircare products you have used and fetch her coat. This will show that you care about the after-service and value her as a customer right up until she leaves. This way your customer won't feel like they are on a conveyer belt in a factory!

After the service

- Always, always when you are building a clientele give them your business card or write your name down on one of the salon appointment cards. They will then remember who to ask for when they re-book and will remember to tell their friends who did their hair.

- If you keep record cards (usually more applicable to colour/perm services), maybe note down something about the customer's visit, e.g. just got married, going on honeymoon, started new job, etc. This will be a talking point when your customer does return to you and she will again feel the personal, caring service of someone who remembers and takes an interest in them.

When customers are nervous

- If the customer is nervous about having their hair done (it could be they have long hair and haven't been to a hair salon for years, or that they've had a bad experience in the past) make sure you use visuals to understand their inter pretation of hair length, colour, types of perm, etc*.

- Don't start suggesting things that you think would suit your customer but would probably be too drastic on this occasion. Building a clientele is about being skilled enough to build your customer's confidence - then you can start to suggest a different colour or a new style. They will trust you more if you do what they want rather than what you want - even if it means that there isn't a big difference in style on the first occasion.

- Talk the customer through what you are doing, e.g. show them the section of hair you are about to cut and by how much.

- Show them how to handle their hair themselves, e.g. advise them on the products you have used and why. Show them how to blow-dry/naturally dry their hair so they can do it themselves at home.

Remember your communication methods. When the customer is nervous, remember to be relaxed and unrushed. Listen clearly as to why she is nervous, e.g. if she has experienced a "scissor happy" hairdresser in the past, reassure her by saying that you will show her the sections and lengths of hair you will be cutting, so she can voice her concerns then if it's too much. Explain that you can just trim the hair today - it doesn't have to be a complete restyle! Use your relaxed, open body language, calm voice and use terminology she will be familiar with.

When customers are unhappy

- If you have done what you agreed at the consultation stage but your customer is unsure, it could be that they need time to get used to the change, e.g. if it is a restyle or a change in colour. Sometimes the customer, even though they've asked for or agreed to a certain look, will need time to get used to seeing themselves differently. They may also want and need the approval and compliments of their partner and friends.
- I would always suggest that you explain to the customer that they have a couple of days to readjust to themselves and if they are still unsure after that, to call you for another appointment.
- If they do re-book, don't see this as an inconvenience; see it as an opportunity to prove to your customer that you are committed to giving her the best service. If it is a lack of communication or a misunderstanding on you part, you will need to provide the service again free of charge; but if you have done exactly what you both agreed, it is acceptable to charge for having to redo the service.

Remember that there is no greater confidence boost than being told how good you look! Sometimes a change in colour or hair length can be a shock - even if you think you are prepared. Having time away from the salon will give your customer the chance to seek the approval/confidence boost they need.

Colleagues

These relationships will lead to friendships and will enhance a positive, friendly atmosphere in the salon you work in.

It is the people, as well as the place and salary, who make us want to go to work in the morning. Customers will also pick up on a relaxed, happy environment and this will enhance their visit. There is nothing worse than walking into a tense atmosphere with moody and miserable staff. Imagine how you would feel if you were seated in a restaurant and you heard the waiters and waitresses bickering or standing around bitching while you were waiting to be served. What if you could hear shouting coming from the kitchen? This would have an impact on how relaxing and pleasurable your experience would be. Would this be a place you would like to eat in again?

Hopefully you will work within a salon where there is mutual respect for everyone. If you do come across conflicts, it could be short-term if maybe an existing member of staff feels threatened by a new member. If this is the case, usually with time it resolves as everyone finds his or her role and place in the salon pecking order. If it is a conflict that is affecting the morale of everyone else or that customers can see and hear, then a well-respected member of staff may want to point this out in the staff room. If the hint is not taken then the salon manager will need to be made aware of it and deal with the root of the issue.

Conclusion

Relationships are important and need to be managed. You are in a people-oriented industry where your customers are your salary and your colleagues become your friends.

Chapter Eight

Terminology

Hair

Crown - the top of your head.

Nape - the base of your neck where your hair starts.

Hairline - the start of your hair around the face. This is usually finer (thinner) and slightly lighter in colour.

Occipital bone - the bone that protrudes about two and a half inches above your nape. We can use this bone as a guide when cutting so that we achieve a style that works around the head shape.

Parting - hair will naturally fall either side of the parting, which is at the top of the head. We use this to guide us when cutting and colouring so that both sides are even.

Hair structure - layers of protein (keratin) that make up the individual hair, condition, texture and porosity (all explained in Chapter Nine).

Styling

Setting - temporarily moulding the hair around a setting roller (using plastic rollers secured to the head with a long plastic pin). This gives body and lift to a hairstyle.

Velcro rollers - large, light setting curlers that allow the hair to stick to them. This is quicker than plastic rollers and more comfortable for the customer.

Setting lotion - applied to wet or damp hair before setting to help stiffen the hair slightly to prolong the hairstyle.

Blow-drying - using a hairdryer and brush/fingers to give body and shape to a hairstyle.

Body - lift and fullness; gives a thicker appearance.

Texture - wave or curl to the hair so it isn't poker straight (blow-drying, styling with fingers and perms will achieve this).

Colour

Pigment - natural colour found in skin and hair.

Artificial pigment - hair colourant made by manufacturers to change the natural hair pigment*.

Peroxide - activator mixed with permanent hair colour and bleaches.

Ammonia - ingredient in permanent colour and perm lotions, which helps to open the hair so the product can work inside.

Depth - how light or dark the hair is.

Tone - how warm (golden or red tones) or cool (ashen tones) the natural colour is.

Grey - hair that has lost its pigment.

Perm

Curler - small sections of hair are wrapped around this during the permanent wave process.

Perm solution - liquid product specially formulated to change the hair shape.

Neutraliser - fixes the hair's new shape when the perm solution has developed.

Development - set, or suggested, time for perm lotion and colour to work effectively on the hair.

Over-processing - solution that has been left too long on the hair. This can result in dry, frizzy perms.

Conclusion

You will come across different terminology, which will depend on the college/salon you train in. When dealing with colour, you will come across different numbering systems and formulations; none are wrong - just different variations.

Chapter Nine

Understanding hair, colour and perms

Hair itself
Hair is a strong fibre consisting of usually three layers. It is the condition of these layers which tells us if the hair is smooth and shiny or dry and dull - or a combination of both. The three layers that make up our hair are the cuticle, cortex and medulla.

Cuticle
This is the outer layer of the hair, which is made of scales that encircle the hair fibre. The function is to protect the inside of the hair. These scales open and close when the hair is wet or receiving chemical treatments such as colour and perm. Ideally the cuticle layer should lay flat.

Cortex
The inside of the hair, where the chemical changes take place. When perming, the sulphur bonds are restructured so that the hair mirrors the shape of the curler permanently. When colouring takes place, the natural pigment is changed or removed and artificial pigment is added.

Natural moisture is also found in the cortex, which is why it's important to keep the cuticle in good condition, as when the scales are flat they are keeping the moisture inside. When hair loses its moisture it becomes brittle and breaks.

Medulla

This is not present in all hair types. It is usually found in coarser hair and is the central layer. There is no known function of the medulla!

Condition

When hair is in good condition it looks shiny, feels smooth and is easier to cope with as it is less tangled and the colour is likely to last longer. This is because the cuticle layer is flat and allows light to bounce off the surface, which creates shine and promotes healthy-looking hair. When the cuticle is damaged by excessive blow-drying or misuse of colour or perm treatments, the cuticle will be raised (or even missing in places). Light will not be reflected, but will be absorbed, which means the hair will look duller.

If the cuticle is damaged it will not be able to protect the inside of the hair as well, and therefore moisture and colour can be lost when shampooing. This is when hair becomes dryer and colour fades quicker.

Texture

This is the diameter of the hair (fine or coarse hair). Finer hair will have fewer cuticles and a smaller cortex. Coarser hair will have more layers of cuticle and a bulkier cortex.

The reason we need to understand this is that coarser hair can be more resistant, especially when perming, and so we need to select the correct strength of product.

Porosity

This is the hair's ability to absorb moisture, including hair colourants and perm solutions. Porous hair is usually finer or damaged hair and needs to be treated more gently.

Colour pigment (depth and tone)

Black, brown, red and yellow pigment is found naturally within the cortex. The darker the hair, the more black and brown pigment; the lighter the hair, the less black and brown pigment. The amount of red and yellow will give the natural colour its tone (how warm or cool).

If you have a close look at someone with naturally brown hair, you will see that it is not a solid colour. There will be glints of tone, e.g. slightly red strands. These natural pigments are removed or changed by permanently colouring the hair. Semi-permanent colours or colour-staining, which affects the cuticle only, will not interfere with natural colour pigment.

Everyone's natural colour will fall into one of the following descriptions.

Depth (how light or dark we are):
- Black (mainly black and brown pigment).
- Dark brown.
- Medium brown.
- Light brown.
- Dark blonde.
- Medium blonde.
- Light Blonde.
- Very light blonde.
- Lightest blonde (less black and brown pigments).

Tone (how warm or cool we are):
- Ashen (no visible gold or red).
- Golden (more yellow pigment).
- Copper (more red and yellow pigment).

The rules of colour are always the same. E.g. if you mix red and yellow paint together, you will get orange. In hairdressing terms, we call this copper.

Colour
The colour star
In colouring we use the colour star as a guide:

Yellow

Green ↖ ↑ ↗ Orange

Grey

Blue ↙ ↓ ↘ Red

Purple/Violet

The reasons we need to learn this are:
- Opposite colours subdue or counteract each other e.g.:
  - Red and green counteract.
  - Purple/violet and yellow counteract.
  - Blue and orange counteract.
  - The colour star is made up of primary and secondary colours.
  - Primary colours cannot be made and are stronger - red, yellow, blue.

- Secondary colours are made by mixing together the primary colours:

  red and yellow = orange
  red and blue = purple/violet
  blue and yellow = green.

- We need to know which colours to mix together to achieve the desired effect (a bit like if we were using paints).
- Yellow and red = orange (we call this copper in hairdressing terms). More red than yellow = red-orange (red copper); more yellow than red = yellow orange (golden copper).
- Red and blue = purple/violet (we call this mahogany in hairdressing terms). More red than blue = purple (mahogany tones); more blue than red = violet (claret, cooler tones).
- Blue and yellow = green (this is an ashen colour and would have been used to counteract red: however, there are other quicker methods now).
- Grey sits in the centre of the colour star. This is a neutral colour. If you were mixing paint, you would mix all six colours of the colour star together in varying amounts (as some colours are more dominant than others, e.g. blue is stronger than yellow). Remember art classes in school? Did you ever have the jam jar of water to swill your brushes in as you changed colours? After a while it turned a cloudy grey colour as the colours in the water all counteracted each other.

Types of colour

Temporary colour
Usually in mousse or setting lotion form. It stains the outer layer of the hair (cuticle) and usually only lasts for one shampoo. Temporary colours do not have chemicals that lighten the hair and they are therefore in natural or red shades.

Semi-permanent/toners/rinses
These last for anything up to ten shampoos but again contain no chemicals and therefore do not lighten the hair. They add a richer tone to the natural colour and add condition.

Quasi-colour
In between a semi-permanent and permanent colour. They do not completely shampoo from the hair, but are designed to fade gradually. These are good for adding stronger tone, e.g. red or darker shades. These will cover a percentage of grey but will not lighten the hair.

Permanent colour/tint
This is mixed with hydrogen peroxide, which breaks down the artificial colour molecules. Ammonia is an ingredient of permanent colour as it helps to open the cuticle to allow the colour to work inside the hair. Once inside the cortex, the colour molecule expands, making it too large to seep out of the cuticle and therefore becoming permanent.

Permanent colour will lighten, darken, add tone and cover grey hair 100%. We can use it for highlights and other colour techniques because it has a thicker consistency, rather than semi-permanents which are usually runnier.

Bleach

This is a lightening product only. It will not darken or add a different tone to the hair. It is excellent for light blonde highlights or an all-over, creamy white blonde effect. It is also good for colour corrections, e.g. a permanent colour that is too dark and needs lifting. Tint will not lift tint, which is why bleach is used more commonly for colour corrections.

Perming

Sulphur bonds

Imagine the rungs of a ladder. These are similar to the way the sulphur bonds are arranged in the cortex. The solution breaks the links and reforms them to the shape of the curler.

Perm lotion

Permanent wave solution soaks into the hair, preferably without dripping onto the scalp. This is developed for usually twenty to forty minutes. During this time the sulphur bonds change to mirror the shape of the curler. When the hair has taken on the shape of the curler, the hair is rinsed at the back-wash (with the curlers still in). Neutraliser is then applied which fixes the curl in place. Usually ten minutes' development is sufficient before the curlers are removed without pulling the hair. You should see crisp curls.

- Small curls will be achieved by using small curlers.
- Open, more natural curls can be achieved with two sizes of curler: larger ones for the open curls and slightly smaller ones to give support. If a perm is too soft then it can relax (drop) very quickly.
- Wavy hair will be achieved with the largest curlers and works best on short and medium-length hair. Too large a curler on long heavy hair will result in a flat, floppy perm,

as the weight of long hair will drag it down. This is why in the consultation process you need to be realistic as to what the customer can achieve on their hair type/style.

Afro-Caribbean hair

Afro-Caribbean hair can be cut and styled to create a shape that will work around and complement the head shape. We can also relax (straighten) or perm on large curlers to smooth the naturally curly texture.

A popular method of cutting for this texture is freehand. This is an unstructured haircut (meaning that we do not follow set technical sections or patterns). Freehand is a very skilled form of cutting, where we work with the natural texture by eye.

Relaxer

This is a specialist straightening chemical product, which is applied carefully to the hair. It is usually a thick crème that will not drip onto the scalp. Once applied to the hair, we can start to smooth down the hair until it looks straight. There is a development time and neutralising process to ensure it is permanent. There are specialist Afro-Caribbean salons that are expert in dealing with these products and hair types.

Summary
Hair

Cuticle, cortex and medulla. Imagine the layers of a pencil: the paint outside is the shiny, protective layer; the inside is the cortex; and the medulla is the lead that runs through the centre.

Condition

The product is only as good as the hair it's on. If colours fade dramatically, it will be due to bad condition or too harsh after-care products. Remember, if the cuticle is open or missing due to damage, it cannot protect the inner hair, which is when moisture and colour can seep out.

Texture and porosity

How fine, coarse and receptive the hair is to colour and perm treatments. Perms can be frizzy due to over-processing, because the solution is too strong or has been overdeveloped. Porous hair is like a sponge; dip a sponge in red paint and it soaks it up; keep squeezing it under a tap and it gradually fades.

Depth and tone

Black, brown, red, yellow colour found naturally in our hair. The more black or brown, the darker the hair; the less black or brown, the lighter the hair.

Colour star

The rules of colour are the same, whether it be hair colouring, painting, make-up, etc. Remember - opposites counteract or subdue each other and we can make new colours by mixing variations together.

Temporary colour

Stains the cuticle. Last until the next shampoo.

Semi-permanent colour

Stains the cuticle. Lasts for up to ten shampoos.

Quasi-colour
Doesn't completely shampoo away but fades and leaves no definite regrowth.

Permanent colour/tint
This will change the natural colour pigment within the cortex, e.g.:

* Darker hair to golden blonde.
* Darker hair to light copper.
* Medium brown hair to black, red, or lighter, golden blondes.
* Lighter hair to black, reds, paler blondes.

The more natural pigment we have, the harder it is to lift the hair to blonde, especially if it is very dark or black. This is because darker hair has more pigment to remove. To achieve lighter blondes on dark hair or to correct permanent colours that are too dark, we will need to use bleaching products.

Bleach
Lightening product only, removing natural and artificial colour pigment. Bleach can be used for highlights (pieces of colour in foil/mesh) or as a full head application. When dealing with colour correction - e.g. hair that is coloured too dark or blonde hair that has a slight green tinge - a weaker formulation of bleach can be used to minimise damage to the hair.

Sulphur bonds
These are the hair's structure and are changed by perm lotion to make straight hair wavy or curly.

Perm

A chemical solution that breaks down the sulphur bonds found in the cortex. This makes the hair mirror the shape of the curler it is wrapped around. A neutraliser will fix the newly formed curl so that it is permanently waved.

Relaxer

A chemical crème that adheres to Afro-Caribbean hair and allows us to smooth and straighten the hair permanently.

Try this

* Take a few strands of your hair and run your index finger and thumb from the root (closest to the scalp) to the end (tip). How does it feel? Rough? Smooth? Smooth at the root and rough towards the end?
* This will tell you the state of the cuticle layer. When hair feels rougher, the cuticles are slightly raised*.
* Feel the diameter of the strands of hair. Are they very thin and soft? Are they slightly rougher and coarser? This tells you the texture. The texture is the diameter of the individual hair, not the amount - e.g. someone can have very fine hair in texture but a lot of it.
* Have a good close look at your family's and friends' hair. Look at the natural colour. Can you see a very flat, ashen (mousy) tone? Are there glints of gold or red? Remember, natural colour is not a solid colour. We need to be aware of this when we are lightening the natural colour. The more warm pigment we have in our hair, the harder it is to lighten. In some cases, the hair can lift up to orange or yellow. As a colourist, you will become skilled in choosing colours that lighten the natural colour and counteract warm tones, so you can achieve paler blondes, for example.

- Get used to thinking about colour descriptions that will make hair colour sound appealing to your future customers, e.g.:
  - Reds - chestnut red, copper red, strawberry blonde.
  - Purples - damson, claret red, mahogany red.
  - Brown - rich, warm brown, golden brown, dark chocolate brown.
  - Blonde - golden honey blonde, pale honey blonde, beige blonde.
  - Notice anyone with naturally curly hair? How do the curls look? Tight? Wavy? Usually, naturally curly hair is a mixture of wavy, straighter and curly pieces; it is very rarely a uniform tight set of curls. When customers want a natural effect, you will need to use your skills as a permer by using different curler sizes and techniques.

Chapter Ten

Understanding haircutting and the tools you will need

Hair growth patterns

There are 90,000 to 140,000 hairs that grow on the average head. These do not all grow in the same direction. This is why you sometimes have one side of your hair that is slightly thicker or that doesn't sit quite as well as the other side! Sometimes we may have a very strong swirl of growth, especially near the crown, which we must be aware of and treat with care when cutting. We need to work with growth patterns rather than trying to force the hair to sit in a way that it doesn't want to, otherwise we will cut it one way but it will spring back in the opposite direction.

Hairline

Again, we cannot force the hairline to sit in a certain way, but what we can do is recommend a hairstyle that complements the growth. E.g. a cowlick is a section of hair by the forehead that has a strong area of growth, usually growing backwards. To have a fringe would be working against the way the hair wants to grow. It would be better cutting a style where the hair was swept back or to the side of the forehead.

The hairline in the nape can also have strong growth, e.g. if the hairline is flat then long, short or graduated cuts are suitable. If there is strong growth inward at sides where the hairline almost jumps up, then a medium or longer style may be suitable.

One-length haircuts

Long hair is usually classed as hair touching or below the shoulders. When the hair is all one length from the sides to the back, this is classed as one length. Examples of one-length hairstyles are the classic and ever-popular bob, which can be neck length or just above shoulder length.

Long/medium layered haircuts

This is where there is a nice strong shape, e.g. the outline of a bob, with layers cut to complement the shape of the head. Layers on the right hair type can give extra body when blow-drying or support a perm better than long hair will. Layers can give the hair a fuller texture, especially if the hair is straight.

Short layered haircuts

These look fabulous on girls and boys. Short haircuts are layered haircuts that again complement the head shape. Hair that's short can look textured and choppy with the right styling products and can give a very fashionable look.

Graduated haircuts

Very clever haircuts, which start off shorter in the nape and gradually get longer towards the occipital and crown areas. This gives an effect of the hair gradually getting longer, which, cut the right way, looks blended and complements the curves of the head.

Club cutting

A section of hair is taken and then the index and forefinger run along it until reaching the desired amount to be cut. Club cutting is cutting in a straight, blunt line. You would use this for a one-length haircut, for example.

Texturing/feather cutting

This is where you chip into the hair with your scissors. This will create a blended look or a more textured style, e.g. with a short layered cut.

Scissor over comb

Used on short hair, e.g. short at the back and sides. It helps the short hair look blended rather than as if chunks of hair have been snipped out.

Freehand cutting

No comb is used. This is for naturally curly and afro hair. This is a very visual technique to personalise a style for the customer. It allows the stylist to create shape, working with the natural curl.

General haircutting rules

Cutting hair must complement the following:

* Head shape.
* Face shape.
* Growth patterns.
* Natural texture.

You must establish how the customer will look after the hairstyle after leaving the salon:

* Do they have time to blow-dry a style every day?
* Do they expect to just shampoo their hair in the morning and leave the house?

A good haircut will not only suit the customer, but will enable them to do their own hair at home. If you have your hair cut and then have it blow-dried into the style you want, it is going to be very difficult for the customer to recreate this look at home. With today's demanding lifestyles for mothers, carers, working men and women, a good haircut that requires little maintenance at home is definitely value for money!!

Excellent examples of hair salons that have "It's the cut that counts" philosophy, are the well-known chains such as Vidal Sassoon and Toni & Guy.

Recommending products

It is part of your professional role to recommend the right products for the customer to use at home. This does not mean you need to give them the hard sell (pressurising the customer into feeling she has to purchase the product). If the customer isn't interested, then he or she will tell you. You will probably find that most customers are grateful for any advice that will save them time and make doing their own hair easier.

Try to ensure that you are familiar with the product categories below so you can recommend with confidence:

* Shampoo and conditioner specific to the customer's hair type.
* Leave-in conditioning mousse.
* Gels, mousse, hairsprays.
* Heat protection sprays, protein sprays.
* Sun-care products for holidays.

Buying signals

Be aware of "buying signals", which we touched on in Chapter Five. Buying signals could include the following:

* If a customer shows interest by asking your opinion on what he or she should use.

- If the customer starts reading the back of the bottle.
- If the customer asks you how he or she should recreate their style at home.
- If the customer complains that her hair is dry or that colour fades, curls look fluffy/frizzy, etc.
- If the customer asks how much the product costs.

Tools you will need

The equipment you will need is listed below. This will enable you to deal with all hair types and hairdressing requests. You will need to carry your equipment in a tool roll (compartments you slide your combs and brushes into and then roll up) or an equipment box (like a small vanity case).

You can buy the equipment you will need at one of the larger hairdressing wholesalers or hopefully the salon or college will order them in and sell them to you at a discounted rate!

- A quality pair of professional hairdressing scissors.
- A small-toothed cutting comb for ladies' hairdressing.
- Small-toothed cutting comb for barbering.
- A large-toothed jumbo comb for long hair or detangling wet hair at the back wash.
- A set of Denman hairbrushes for blow-drying (small, medium and large).
- A good hairdryer.
- A diffuser (attachment that fits at the end of the hairdryer to spread out heat). This would be used for naturally curly or newly permed hair.
- Sectioning clips.
- Colouring gloves
- Needle comb/pintail comb (used for weaving hair when highlighting).

- Tint bowl and brush (these are plastic, washable and do not bleach or stain).
- Various sized curlers (if you are freelance or a mobile hairdresser).
- Various sized Velcro setting rollers. These are used for setting and will stay secure in the hair while it dries. This is quicker and more comfortable for the customer than the old plastic-and-pin rollers.
- A selection of styling products (if you are a mobile hairdresser).
- You will also need a steriliser. It is essential that your equipment is clean and sterilised after every use.

Summary

Growth patterns
Different directions the hair will grow in, e.g. the crown may have a strong swirl of growth, meaning that the hair around it will grow strongly to the left, right, backwards or forwards.

One-length haircuts
Hair all the same length. This is for medium and long hair (hair below the shoulders).

Layers
A hairstyle which has differing lengths - short, medium and long.

Graduation
A style which may be shorter in the nape and gradually builds up to being longer.

Tools

Needed to cut, colour, perm, blow-dry and style the hair.

Try this

- Look at your family's and friends' hair close up. Look at the crown and observe how it grows. Look at the hairlines, above the forehead and especially in the nape. Again, observe how they grow and what style would complement (or not complement!) their growth patterns.
- Pick out, quietly to yourself, which are one-length haircuts, which have layers and which are short. Look at the way the haircuts work around the shape of the head.
- Visit the nearest hairdressing wholesaler or ask any hairdressing friends about the cost of the tools you will need. You can then plan a budget as to what you can afford and prioritise which you buy first, e.g. scissors, comb, hairdryer and steriliser.

Finally

Looking after you!

Your health is important. When you get your first full- or part-time job as a hairdresser, be sure to take care of yourself.

- Eat as normally as you can. It is not uncommon for hairdressers to work all through the day with no breaks, breakfast or lunch. Your employer should give you a morning and afternoon break as well as time off for lunch if you are working a full day, e.g. 8.30 a.m. to 6.00 p.m.
- You can become dehydrated, which will make you tired and sluggish or, in extreme cases, you could end up with something more serious like a stomach ulcer if you don't eat and drink properly.

- Hands can suffer as a result of constant shampooing. A common complaint is dermatitis. This inflames the skin, causing it to chap and be sore (believe me, I've had it!).
- Try to make sure you dry your hands thoroughly after you've finished shampooing. A good crème is E45, which can be bought from your local pharmacy.
- Legs and feet can ache when you first start working in the salon. You will very likely be on your feet most, if not all, of the day.
- Try to wear a full shoe to prevent in-growing toenails. Keep your toenails clipped so they do not dig in, and try to massage your feet with a good moisturiser whenever you can.
- Family, friends and partners can sometimes feel neglected when you start a new career, especially one with long hours. Make sure you still spend quality time with them as well - after all, they will probably be your first models on whom to practise the new techniques you learn!
- Tempers in a busy salon can sometimes fray, especially if the stylist is running late and feeling under pressure. The ones they are likely to snap at are juniors/assistants and receptionists. If you are quite a sensitive person, try not to take this too personally or feel that you have done something wrong. Understand that pressures cause people to snap or shout. Continue with what you are doing and understand that it is the situation talking. This non-reactive approach will help defuse, not aggravate, the situation - you may even get an apology! Sometimes you are a greater person to walk away - even if you don't want to! The hairdressing industry is a "people" industry, and this is part and parcel of dealing with them!

Final word - confidence

Learning takes time. We all learn differently, depending on what our "learning styles" are, e.g.:

+ Do we need someone to explain to us what we need to do and how we are to do it?
+ Do we need to actually "do" to learn and understand?
+ Do we need to write information down to refer back to in order for it to "sink in"?
+ Do we need a combination of understanding the theory, seeing it put into practice and then doing it ourselves? E.g.:
  - We need to understand how semi-permanent colour works (theory).
  - Observe how a colourist chooses and applies the colour (demonstration).
  - Experience choosing and applying the colour ourselves (doing).

Whatever our style, it is knowledge, understanding and experience that will give us confidence. We cannot be expected to feel confident in cutting someone's hair until we understand what needs to be done, what we will take into consideration to achieve the look, and how we will do it. When our customers are happy, this gives us the greatest confidence.

Our confidence can also take knocks though, as we will sometimes come across customer responses such as unsure, unhappy or even tearful. Part of our learning will be how to deal with people and situations and how to correct them.

Quote to remember

"Expect to be in training for two to three years before you qualify."

Index

Websites

www.jhpublications.co.uk

www.cityandguilds.co.uk
enquiry@city-and-guilds.co.uk

www.jhpublications.co.uk
Authors website providing details on the book/ useful links

www.city-and-guilds.co.uk
Providing information on the industry NVQ qualifications

www.vidalsassoon.co.uk

Careers, application forms, seminars, salon directory and company & philosophy.

www.toniandguy.co.uk

Careers, education, products, history & philosophy.

www.wella.co.uk

Company information, products, education support.

www.hairdressersjournal.co.uk

Industry events and news.